Australian Biographical Monographs

5

Australian Biographical Monographs
Series Editor: Scott Prasser

Previous Volumes

1
Joseph Lyons and the Management of Adversity
Kevin Andrews

2
Harold Holt and the Liberal Imagination
Tom Frame

3
Johannes Bjelke-Petersen
Bruce Kingston

4
Lindsay Thompson
Character, Competence and Conviction
William Westerman

Australian Biographical Monographs

5

Neville Wran

David Clune

Connor Court Publishing

Published in 2020 by Connor Court Publishing Pty Ltd

Connor Court Publishing Pty Ltd
PO Box 7257
Redland Bay QLD 4165
sales@connorcourt.com
www.connorcourt.com
Phone 0497-900-685

Printed in Australia

ISBN: 9781922449092

Front cover design: Maria Giordano

Front cover picture: Portrait of Neville Wran, Premier of New South
Wales, 1 January 1970, Wikipedia Commons.

"That's what being in the working class is all about — how to get out of it"

Series overview

Connor Court's *Australian Biographical Series* on past leading Australian political leaders and other important figures seeks to provide an overview for those who are unfamiliar with the subject and to highlight the person's particular importance, controversies, and contributions to Australia's progress.

The monographs are scholarly rather than academic in focus, placing emphasis on a clear narrative, but with careful attention to referencing to ensure views expressed are supported by appropriate sources and evidence.

The Series was initiated because of the decline in the study of Australian history at our schools and universities. Consequently, there has been a lack of knowledge or, even worse, distorted views, of some of Australia's leading historical figures who deserve to be remembered, better understood for their achievements, and, as each volume also highlights, their flaws.

Sir Paul Meernaa Caedwalla Hasluck, KG, GCMG, GCVO, PC, (1 April 1905-9 January 1993) was a senior public servant, diplomat, academic, federal member of the House of Representatives from 1949-69, held several key ministries and then served as Governor-General from 1969-74. Hasluck was not just an office holder, he mastered them. More than that he made important by his work and insights what was then regarded as minor ministries like Territories, appreciating the plight of our Aboriginal people and those in New Guinea. He acted, pushed and reformed. His many publications on Australian history and its institutions were, and are, highly regarded. A man of high ethical principles, nurtured by his strong Salvation Army background which he remained true to all this life, Hasluck stood out from our usual perceptions of politicians – then and now. And yet, for all this, and despite several significant biographies, Hasluck is almost forgotten especially among his own party. This makes this latest monograph by Anne Henderson, the 26th in the *Australian Biographical Series*, timely in reminding us not just what Hasluck achieved, but when decency mattered.

Anne Henderson is deputy director of the Sydney Institute and has been a major contributor to promoting the study of Australian politics through her many publications including another in this series on Senator Margaret Guilfoyle.

- Scott Prasser

(Editor, Australian Biographical Monographs)

PAUL HASLUCK

Anne Henderson

Paul Meerna Caedwalla Hasluck entered Australia's federal parliament in December 1949 on the incoming tide of freshly elected members of Robert Menzies' victorious Liberal Party as representative for the new seat of Curtin in Perth. Aged 44, he carried an unusual full name. His second name of "Meerna", passed down from his paternal grandfather, derived from an Aboriginal word meaning joyful spring of fresh water. This combined in unique ways with "Caedwalla" of Anglo-Saxon heritage.

Hasluck had entered federal parliament after a successful professional life as a journalist for *The West Australian* and later as an officer in the Department of External Affairs, urged on by a recommendation from Labor leader John Curtin, including as Australia's first Permanent Representative to the United Nations from 1946 to 1947. As a writer and historian, Hasluck would publish two volumes of the official history of Australia's involvement in World War II and work briefly as an academic at the University of Western Australia.

This newly elected MP, however, had passions unusual for his time. Within six months of taking his seat, Hasluck rose in the House on 8 June 1950 to move a motion of some length. The motion opened with these words:

> That this House is of the opinion that the Commonwealth Government, exercising a national responsibility for the welfare of the whole Australian people, should co-operate with the State Governments in measures for the social advancement as well as the protection of people of the Aboriginal race throughout the Australian mainland.[2]

In arguing for his motion, Hasluck acknowledged the deep frustration among "native administrators, government departments and Aboriginal welfare associations" at the conditions Australia's diverse groups of Indigenous people lived with. He was not casting blame but spoke of how the "neglect of this social problem in the past has been neglect on the part of the Australian community as a whole". His motion sought to "arouse the Australian nation to some sense of its responsibility for its shortcomings in this matter". Hasluck spoke of his work with the Moseley Commission in 1934-35 examining the conditions of life of Western Australian Aboriginals, reports of which he had published in *The West Australian*. He noted that 16 years later, the numbers of half castes in the regions Moseley investigated had grown by 50 per cent and yet their condition was "far worse than it was in 1934 just after the depression".

For the time, this stand by the new MP for Curtin would mark him out as one of a kind. Aboriginal policy and its attention from government was at its nadir for state governments and largely ignored by the federal administration. It was left, as Hasluck opined, at "the tail-end of the proceedings of the various conferences… [and] treated as one of the left-overs."[3] Tellingly, Hasluck biographer Geoffrey Bolton has written that "Aboriginal policy was one of the major themes of Hasluck's public career".[4] Hasluck himself, in one of his last speeches, spoke of Australian Aboriginals, their welfare and their status as Australians, as one of his three chief interests over 65 years.[5]

Paul Hasluck MP was no ordinary individual but, over

time, his many achievements have faded in the historical memory. Former Western Australian premier Sir Charles Court, in his introduction to *Paul Hasluck in Australian History*, writes that Hasluck might have been prime minister after Harold Holt drowned in late 1967. Sir Robert Menzies convinced Hasluck to have a go. "Did he want it?" asks Court. "We may never know."[6] Interviewed by Gerard Henderson in the early 1990s, Hasluck explained how he did not canvas colleagues as he challenged John Gorton for the leadership. He was not "competitive" and had never had any ambition to get into politics which "just happened" when he was approached. His lack of ambition in seizing the top job in 1968 disappointed most members of the Cabinet and other significant members of the party when he lost narrowly.[7]

Academic Richard Nile, who brought together a host of leading intellectuals to write about Paul Hasluck in 1999, captured the essence of the influences on Hasluck in his political life: "The great influences ... were H.V. Evatt as a model of what not to be, John Curtin as a man who gave himself to the service of the nation, and Robert Menzies, the politician he most admired and whom he served faithfully even during twelve years of great doubting as the Minister for Territories".[8] Of Robert Menzies, Hasluck would reflect, years later, "...the sort of tribute he would have appreciated most would not have been praise of his great talents but rather a statement that he was a man of character, honourable in conduct and decent in behaviour. He was that".[9] In this summing up, there is much to be seen of Paul Hasluck himself.

Paul Hasluck might have had a fairly ordinary middle

class upbringing had his English born father not found God at the age of 18 while comfortably employed at the Colonial Post Office. As a Salvation Army officer, Hasluck's father Meerrna Hasluck met and married Hasluck's mother Patience Eliza Wooler, a young woman who had come to Western Australia from England to take up the position of companion to Mrs Hare, wife of the resident magistrate. Miss Wooler had converted to the Salvation Army while working with the Hares.

Paul Hasluck has written that "the fact that my father was in the Salvation Army had so much to do with my own life … I never saw any sign that questioning or doubt entered his own mind. The dedication behind 'trust and obey' was complete … My father had an unquestioning faith; my mother had an unquestioning duty of helping others".[10] In time, Hasluck would reflect that his family's religious values had "produced the habit of examining and questioning my own conduct". He could sense this explained a lot about his choices and attitudes in life, writing, "An introspective man is not disqualified from action but sometimes he may be handicapped".[11]

Apart from that sense of duty, instilled in Hasluck as a child and which he realised carried over for the rest of his life, living in the various Salvation Army quarters offered the young Hasluck a host of experiences not usual in a middle class home. The family had little money and in his teenage years he sought all manner of odd jobs to help financially. For all that, an unexpected chance to see more of the world came to Paul by way of his father's allegiance to God. Meerrna Hasluck was selected to attend a Salvation Army world congress in London lasting two months during England's summer of 1914.

Meerrna was allowed to take one family member. The family selected nine-year-old Paul since his older brother Lewis had been in England as an infant and his mother had to stay home to run the Salvation Army Boys' Home they were in charge of. It was a watershed moment for the young Hasluck. A sea voyage to London of itself was broadening. In London, while Meerrna soaked up the Salvation Army's massed meetings and processions, Paul revelled in famous tourist sights from the Tower of London to Windsor Castle and Westminster, along with Tussaud's waxworks.[12]

As a young boy, Hasluck lived in a Salvation Army centre at Collie, at a boys home his parents ran 200 kilometres south of Perth, where he mucked about with local lads, some of them Aboriginal, learned to ride and developed a love of horses. In the early 1940s while he worked at the Department of External Affairs in Canberra, his black thoroughbred mare Edythe, stabled unlawfully in the back yard of his Canberra cottage, would munch on grass at Camp Hill and then take him home for a quick lunch.

Hasluck never lost his love for the unspoiled bush. In his retirement, especially, and in other moments of relaxation, he spent many of his days in a small dwelling he had built on 60 acres, inland from Perth in the Darling Range, where he listened to classical music, cooked meals and retreated among the song birds and smell of eucalypts. In "A Footnote to the Last Poem in the Book", he wrote of listening to Palestrina "in the still hush of noon, looking out on gumtrees, blackboys, zamia palms and the mingled green and brown of untouched forest with brilliant patches of blue sky beyond". To him, the sound and the setting enhanced each other, to which he added: "A century or two ago, people who thought of such music felt like exiles sad and sick for home. I listen to it feeling that it belongs to my home".[13]

In time, having won a scholarship and with the broadening experience of spending five years completing his secondary education at the Perth Modern School, Hasluck would lead something of a double life. An avid reader of the classics and advanced literature, his respect for his parents could not extinguish his abhorrence at what he termed "the hot-gospelling and the public practice of religion".[14] Then, at 17, his father helped him obtain a position with *The West Australian*, Perth's morning daily, after meeting its proprietor in the street. This was a leap into the modern. Journalism not only offered Hasluck a freedom to attain the self-education he sought, it also opened wider horizons.

Yet, Hasluck's Salvation Army background would stay in his DNA. After a stressful and unimpressive performance in July 1965, at a Monash University teach-in up against Dr Jim Cairns, debating Australia's commitment to the Vietnam War, Hasluck showed a tendency to bad temper in some of his public appearances in the months that followed. A lack of control under internal pressure. As this reputation grew, it was on a quiet night around 2 am in the chamber when deputy opposition leader Gough Whitlam lost control and emptied a glass of water over Hasluck who had simply come into the House to advise the minister in charge of the discussion that debate would be adjourned. The bill under discussion included exempting Salvation Army officers working with the armed services from being eligible for armed services pensions. As Whitlam hounded government MPs for their lack of interest in speaking on the bill, Hasluck joined Country Party whip Winton Turnbull in interjecting that this was not true. This led Whitlam to gibe at Hasluck that he was "prepared to deny his parents" in supporting the legislation. At this, Hasluck responded that Whitlam was "one of the filthiest objects ever to come into this chamber".[15] The water incident followed. Apologies came thick and fast.[16]

It would be Alix Hasluck who could explain something of her husband's behaviour under pressure. The couple had met when Hasluck was completing a Diploma of Journalism at the University of Western Australia. Alix Drucker, then a third-year student, was the producer of a performance of *Everyman* and Paul Hasluck had been given the role of Everyman. Their literary interests clicked – and their sense of humour. As Peter Ryan, who came to know Hasluck as a close friend in his later life, wrote in his biological cameo on Hasluck, Paul's outer demeanour in public life gave no glimpse of "the positively mischievous sense of fun" he had.[17] The couple married on 14 April 1932 and spent a year following their wedding touring the UK and Europe thanks to a small legacy Alix had inherited. This was an unusual couple – dedicated to broadening their experience of both history and culture beyond the small settlement of Perth and beyond the isolated global setting of their home continent. In the UK, they spent weeks researching their various interests in the British Museum and for ten weeks Hasluck volunteered with two missions to the slums.[18] Hasluck also used some of his savings to attend two summer schools of the League of Nations held in Geneva.

But their life together quickly forced Alix to a tactful understanding that her husband had some strange habits. In her memoir she described how it was:

> I had discovered almost immediately after the wedding that Paul had a very bad temper, of a sort that was completely beyond my ken … It took me many years to find that though his anger seemed to be directed at me, it often had nothing to do with me but related to some incident several days before on which he had been brooding. I was only the catalyst. And he suffered from severe migraines … All this made for some very dark times when Paul would savagely fling off on his own, leaving me in a strange city not only alone, for I did not mind that much, but unknowing what had become of him.[19]

Alix Hasluck, in time a prolific writer herself, would be the longstanding and perfect companion for Paul Hasluck, ready to move house from Perth to Canberra or further afield to New York city, at a moment, while also spending many months alone caring for the Haslucks' two sons Rollo (born January 1941) and Nicholas (born October 1942) as her husband travelled overseas for conferences to set up the United Nations and, later, as the Minister for Territories. All this, especially, at a time when Perth was a most distant spot on the Australian map. As well, Alix offered Hasluck the intellectual backup he needed. He would call her and chat from far away, and write to her, and her advice was taken seriously.

In public life, Hasluck would always throw off a formal style, meticulous and dutiful. But in private and in moments of relaxation he could be both a bit of a larrikin and an entertainer. He could command an audience with a performance on native drums and in Washington in 1942, when he was spending Christmas with an American family, he joined in the renditions, singing bass for "Way Down Upon the Swanee River" and "Camptown Races" to the extent that his hosts delighted he knew such songs and their singing went on into the small hours.[20] Living in Canberra in the early 1940s, food and essentials were hard to come by – much less a keg of beer. It would be Paul Hasluck who put his horse Edythe in shafts to help salvage a nine-gallon barrel of beer from a Queanbeyan publican needing to save his war time quota. With Alix away in Perth, Hasluck and his mates made good use of the nine gallons.[21] And it was Paul Hasluck, as the very proper External Affairs Minister in 1964, who had his prime minister, Robert Menzies, bring back his gift from the Indonesians on the prime ministerial RAAF plane - a stuffed tiger which Hasluck presented to the Claremont Football Club, called "the Tigers", where it became their mascot and still resides today.

Tackling the record

It may have been by chance and the need to support himself with a reasonable regular income that Paul Hasluck, aged 18, found himself working as a journalist. But the job suited him in so many ways. He loved the chance to dig and probe for stories and even found himself dreaming of being another Dickens, as he put it, "getting material for the great work".[22] He also found he could be interested in the details behind the smallest of stories from a milkmen's strike to the problems faced by the Housewives Association or the differences between Presbyterians and Baptists after listening to a Saturday debate or the state of brothels in the red light district. He worked on the police round and the courts and also got close to the union movement and eventually John Curtin, then editing the *Westralian Worker*. He became a sympathetic unionist himself as a journalist.

This interest in keeping the record took Hasluck into more and more digging when he joined the Western Australian Historical Society in his early twenties. A small settlement like Perth, not quite a century old for the non-Indigenous, could look back and almost touch its past. Hasluck would later dismiss oral history as unreliable but in his first major project he began recording the stories of older West Australians. He would write of one occasion: "So I shook hands with a man who had once been handed a biscuit by Thomas Carlyle".[23]

Hasluck's research patched together the settlement history of Western Australia from convicts to strugglers on the land to those in touch with murder to those who had been in John Forrest's exploring party in 1874 along with old timers from successful colonial families. Hasluck's passion lay in his historical curiosity about how and why things happen. And in keeping the record for future generations. This would develop hugely as he became involved more and more with the operation of historical events both as journalist, public servant and politician.

In the early 1930s, the issue of the treatment and living conditions of Western Australia's Indigenous people – then called full blooded and half-caste Aboriginals – took

Paul Hasluck into an area of more immediate concern. Western Australia, as one of Britain's convict settlements from 1829, had offloaded numbers of men onto the shores of a foreign continent where there were few women of similar ethnic background. The consequences were that, inevitably, freed convicts mated with Aboriginal women at the bottom of the social scale. The subsequent generations of part Aboriginal and part convict offspring were largely tolerated as they found their place in society. Paul Hasluck knew numbers of Aboriginal people as he grew up in the Salvation Army homes his parents cared for at Collie and Guildford. He recalled in his memoir that, "They troubled nobody and nobody troubled them in the easy rent-free part nomadic life they preferred".[24]

In the 1920s, there had been an awakening of political consciousness in Western Australia around voices such as that of Katharine Susannah Prichard, whom Hasluck came to know and support, seeking citizenship for half-castes. The Depression, however, saw many of these Aboriginal and part Aboriginal people falling into the protection of the Chief Protector of Aboriginals, who from 1915 was A O Neville. This branch of government oversaw the policy now known as the stolen generation whereby half caste Aboriginal children were taken from their half-caste families into institutional care. In addition, as settlement moved east of the Avon River, many Aboriginal people were forced off native lands and into unhygienic and unresourced camps with their children barred from schools on the grounds of health risk. By the early 1930s, the problems around Aboriginal conditions had become a public concern.

In 1933, Hasluck supported Sister Kate Clutterbuck in

setting up an Anglican orphanage for part-Aboriginal children in need of care. The home was opened at Queen's Park and Sister Kate demanded that the children in her care would not be segregated but would attend local government schools. Sister Kate's initiative was coupled the same year with Mary Montgomerie Bennett's efforts to use her contacts in London to publicise Western Australia's Aboriginal disadvantages.[25]

Such a stirring of political consciences resulted in the Western Australian government setting up, in 1934, a Royal Commission to "Investigate, Report and Advise Upon Matters in Relation to the Condition and Treatment of Aboriginals" in Western Australia. At Perth's local newspaper, journalist Paul Hasluck was quick off the mark – writing a series of articles ahead of the Royal Commission under the pen name of "Polygon". Over three articles on 9-13 March, Hasluck outlined both the history and realities of honourable intentions and "villainous performance". He wrote of lands "rudely seized" and "no systematic attempt to educate them or introduce them to the new civilisation in which they were expected to live". Going on, he opined:

> There are two impressive figures that cannot be overlooked in any consideration of the economic position of the blacks. Of roughly 18,000 natives (half-castes and full bloods) in touch with civilisation in 1932, there were only permits for employment of 3,856. Of the total, under 4,000 were children. This leaves a total of over 10,000 adults in touch with civilisation whose means of existence is rations. The benevolence is commendable, but their economic status is, and on present policy must, permanently be paupers.[26]

Hasluck criticised the widespread acceptance that the Aboriginal race was doomed to extinction and pushed for government to take a serious interest in work towards bringing the local Aboriginals to better adjustment to living as part of the Australian community. As a result of his articles, Hasluck was selected to accompany the Royal Commissioner, Henry Moseley, on his travels and investigations. Hasluck would report to *The West Australian* over those weeks, collecting a record that was worthy of a stand alone publication. The weeks of hearings and visits produced ample evidence that full blood and half caste Aboriginals lived a half-way life between cultures, where their fates were at the dictation of white authorities for minor infringements.

White citizens added their experience, many sympathetic to seeing change and reform. At the Durack stations in the Northern Territory, the commissioner heard how 120 blacks did the work of less than 40 paid whites. Durack advised that payment in money was worthless for his black employees as the Aboriginals "quickly became the victim of other unprincipled people".[27] Work was compensated by provision of lodgings, blankets, clothing, tobacco and medicine and supplies given freely at stores belonging to the stations. They also were given three months each year for their walkabout. Such Aboriginals were adapting at a low level to white ways in the use of horses, maintenance of fences and stock and in general household tasks. Those not under the security of work on a station were living dubious lives. More serious discoveries were that treatment for leprosy and venereal disease was well behind satisfactory. Not only were the cases of leprosy rapidly turning up but treatment in the north required removal to Darwin with holding centres at Broome and Derby lacking in resources to cope.

By mid June, Hasluck had reasonably well informed impressions from the various interviews and investigations of the Moseley Commission. On 21 June, he wrote towards the end of his report: "From what has been seen to date there can be no hesitation in saying that the treatment of blacks is 'humane' but one keeps on feeling every now and then that the 'humaneness' is of the type which the Royal Society for the Prevention of Cruelty to Animals lives to foster."[28] In reports that followed in 1936, Hasluck described appalling living conditions for many Aboriginals and the standard of accommodation as "rather worse than the poorer class of suburban fowl house".[29]

The report of the Moseley Commission in early 1935 was weak in its assessments and largely ineffective. But the concern it showed over the increase of half-castes did refute the notion that the Aboriginal race was dying out. In fact, the race was regenerating, as Hasluck perceived, and as such it provoked the question of how such individuals should be educated and be recognised and respected as part of the Australian community.

In a series of articles, disguised as "Our Special Correspondent", for *The West Australian* in July 1936, Hasluck described not only the plight of half-caste Aboriginals on the fringes of white settlement and cities but also argued that there was a need for suitable education for the children of these families. Farm schooling was one suggestion where a half-caste child could both learn and return from the school day to a "home" rather than a humpy or a nomadic family where the child might not return to the classroom at all.[30] Hasluck had come to what, until the mid-1930s, was the rather radical view that the best future for the many diverse Aboriginal enclaves was assimilation which would bring education and a rise in living standards. Aboriginal Australians would become part of one Australian nation by learning to live as other Australians. In this, he noted how younger Aboriginal people sought more and more to live closer to white settlements and have the cultural amenities of white life.

Explaining how he came to his understanding of best policy for Aboriginal Australians in the 1930s, Hasluck wrote of the context in which he reasoned:

> My basic assumption is that Aborigines are part of the total Australian community. Even if and when present tendencies toward separate development of Aborigines become more potent the Aborigines will still be part of the Australian population. Hence the broad question for the future is a question of the terms of their membership of the Australian community and the relationship to the various groups within that community.[31]

With his experience of Western Australian Aboriginals in the 1930s, Hasluck became a firm believer that only with education and policy designed to bring Indigenous Australians into mainstream society would the problems he witnessed be addressed. He would hold these views even as the Indigenous push for separate identity took off in the late twentieth century. For Hasluck in the 1930s, it was better for Aboriginal Australians to find ways and means to remove themselves from the Chief Protector, and to find ways towards education and the skills needed to find employment. It was his aspiration that this would lead to both a more empowered and functioning Aboriginal Australia.

In 1937, a small beginning to this end was the Lyons Government's conference in April bringing together all state Aboriginal Boards and Protectors. Conclusions of this conference made note of the great diversity of Aboriginal circumstances. For all that, the conference concluded that "the efforts of all State authorities should be directed toward the education at white standards of children of mixed Aboriginal blood, and their subsequent employment under the same conditions as whites with a view to taking their place in the white community on an equal footing".[32]

Global affairs

Hasluck would reflect in his later life how, in the many twists and turns of his professional career, he had not sought each move himself but had taken up someone else's suggestion to him and thus been pushed forward. With the outbreak of the Second World War, in late 1940, while Alix was expecting their first child, Hasluck was considering enlisting. His brother Lewis had enlisted as had his sister Rosa. His career at *The West Australian* in Perth, albeit as international sub-editor, was not contributing much to the war effort and his time as a fill-in academic for the absent Fred Alexander at the university had ended. His post graduate thesis, which would be later published as *Black Australians*, was done and dusted. Then, a chance meeting with John Curtin, Labor federal opposition leader, turned his head in a new direction.

Curtin advised Hasluck to join the Department of External Affairs where they were looking for qualified graduate staff to develop Australian foreign policy – without Hasluck knowing it at the time, Curtin had already put his name forward.[33] Later, Hasluck would leave an incisive account of his years in the department, published as *Diplomatic Witness*. His description of the ten rooms in West Block that housed the department, presided over by Lt-Colonel William Roy Hodgson, and its functioning rituals leave a time-warped picture of process and not much else. Hasluck captures its homely ways:

> It was a rather daggy office. The clerk in charge of records, George Westcott, always had a blue heeler cattle dog under his table. On occasions, to cope with the exigencies of family life in war-time Canberra, other officers would bring in the family dog for a day.[34]

The department that Hasluck entered, however, was about to be shaken by world events and a new minister. Appointed after the fall of the short-lived Fadden Government in October 1941, Bert (Doc) Evatt became Attorney General and External Affairs minister in the new Curtin Government. A former judge of the High Court, Evatt was known as a minister with brains and, as Hasluck and others have recorded, expectations were high in the department that change and action were afoot.

Hasluck himself was not to know how closely he would

work with Evatt in the six years he eventually spent in the department but, as he has written, "Apart from John Burton, his private secretary and two or three other members of his personal staff, there was probably no other official who saw the minister at closer quarters in his foreign affairs work than I did. Certainly, no officer of the department, other than Burton, worked as close to him or travelled as much with him as I did".[35] That closeness would leave a large footprint – not only would Hasluck be the assiduous officer behind much of Evatt's work towards the setting up of the United Nations (doing his devilling, to use a legal term), he was also a shrewd observer and recorder of Evatt's behaviour as an opportunistic and effective player in world affairs but also as a chaotic manager weakened by an overly suspicious mind.

As an aligned but not permanent officer in the department, Hasluck had spent his first year as something of an attachment with no defined administrative role. Evatt would change that, recognising him as the perfect assistant in speech making and research for wider events. In February 1942, at the time of the fall of Singapore, Evatt made his first important speech to parliament – a speech that Hasluck worked on at a side table in Evatt's office.

From the middle of 1942, Hasluck became the officer working direct to Evatt, keeping pace with his demands. He was valued for his capacity for long, hard working hours, the ability to meet deadlines quickly and not to be flustered by the disorder that Evatt created around him. Hasluck recognised that Evatt had an analytical mind rather than a creative one. Hasluck would serve up the papers he had worked over laboriously, then Evatt would improve a draft to the purpose he wanted, amending, deleting and adding. On one occasion, Hasluck recalls how he and Ken Bailey worked for hours on a submission: "It was about midnight when we showed the minister the five or six typed sheets. He seemed only to glance at them, turning them over rapidly and instantly put his finger on the spot: "That is where the argument breaks down." He scrawled his re-drafting and tightened the whole case".[36]

While Alix Hasluck had relocated to Canberra, albeit in time forced back to Perth for a break with the cold of winter, Hasluck was still within a domestic flight home should his family not return. From late 1942, however, the Hasluck family would become used to long separations as Paul Hasluck took up the first of his overseas missions. He was chosen as the department's representative at the December Institute of Pacific Relations conference on post-war settlement to be held at Mont Tremblant, Quebec. He would afterwards spend Christmas in Washington DC. His travel from Australia across the Pacific he described as "novel" and his appointment was the first to break new ground since departmental officers being sent overseas were normally only for diplomatic postings. In his *Diplomatic Witness*, Hasluck gives a detailed and at times ironically amusing account of the journey which captured the laid back and uncertain Australian departure from Brisbane via a bomber to New Caledonia, and thence kangaroo hopping to Fiji, Canton Island and Honolulu and finally San Francisco. From there, in the midst of a freezing winter, Hasluck made it to Washington DC in time to catch a train to Montreal.

The conference introduced Hasluck to international

exchange and opened his mind to challenges facing a post-war world. He found there was no dynamic post-war policy in Britain and advised that he was not sure "British leaders have yet fully appreciated the nature of post-war problems".[37] He returned to Australia well able to brief his minister, especially on possible roles Australia might have in the post-war world. He also came back with a belief that Australia needed not only to stand up for its own interests in a post-war world but that it also could play a significant role in establishing that world, even as a smaller nation. It was a belief that found favour with Doc Evatt.

At the start of 1944, Alix Hasluck and their now two young boys returned from some months in Perth recovering from life in Canberra. The heightened workload that Evatt had by then pushed on to Hasluck is most closely described by Alix. From 17 January to 22 January, Australia was host in Canberra for the Australia-New Zealand Conference. The conference would be headed by the prime ministers of Australia and New Zealand. Alix records in her memoir how her husband was particularly "touchy and tired out". Then the hours labouring for the minister became obvious:

> In January one night Paul did not come home at all. ... at 5am, ... I heard a terse brief explanation of Evatt's requirements and last minute alterations to some document of major importance on which Paul had worked all night, and which had now gone to the typist and Paul must be back in the office at 7 am to vet it before the meeting at 9 am. "What meeting?" I wailed. "Why can't wretched Evatt let you have some sleep. I bet he's been to bed for a few hours! ... Dr Evatt had rapidly found Paul's

brain and capacity for work of great value and to his liking, and had used him more and more."[38]

Alix Hasluck had also noted that the department's John Hood, in trying to close the post-war section, had become jealous of Evatt's use of Paul and was causing the tension reflected in her husband's moods. In time, similar tension arose between Hasluck and the younger, but rising star, John Burton who became Evatt's favourite and covered for him in the chaos.[39]

Some of the tension within the department reflected in these moods had to do with Hasluck's meticulous standards for correct public service operation. The small department with its orderly processes in a small space suddenly had a chaotic minister to whom Hasluck seemed to be increasingly attached for work. He assessed the effect of Evatt on departmental activities as extremely careless leadership. Evatt's bulging coat pockets "were his filing cabinets for all sorts of material and when of necessity he had to empty his pockets he left papers lying all over the place. ... In matters of my own experience when overseas my chief concern was his neglect to keep his own Prime Minister fully informed of what he was doing ... He did not scruple to destroy or withhold papers which might contradict his own story. Some of us would repeat within our own circles a rather feeble pun about drafts being 'doctored'".[40]

From 5 April to 26 June 1945, representatives of 50 nations met for the San Francisco Conference from which, in time, the United Nations would be formed. Evatt chose his own advisers, among whom was Paul Hasluck. They met first in London, grey and damaged with war detritus, for a British Commonwealth Meeting from 4-13 April. This was a meeting to bring together members of the British Commonwealth in advance of the San Francisco gathering. It was at this initial meeting that Evatt impressed Hasluck with how he "managed to get to the heart of the matter so rapidly" by concentrating on questions relating to the United Nations charter.[41] At the San Francisco meetings, Evatt worked the committees and made an impact but he had a team of excellent advisers, equally working flat out. Alan Renouf put it succinctly:

> Hasluck in particular was stretched to the limit …
> he was Dr Evatt's chief advisor on matters relating
> to the United Nations Charter. In addition, he had to
> attend meetings of the vital Executive Committee
> and Co-Ordination Committee, in addition to
> carrying out responsibilities on a main Conference
> Committee on which he had been assigned.[42]

Historian Carl Bridge has added to this assessment in describing the combination of the erratic Evatt and Hasluck's own very ordered and principled view of foreign policy. Hasluck was methodical and believed a nation should define its fundamental interests and pursue them regardless of momentary distractions. Evatt was quite the reverse much of the time. As Bridge writes: "Evatt ran his department like a ramshackle personal fiefdom, or an old fashioned lawyer's office. Staff were at the minister's beck and call … played off against each other … dependent on the minister's patronage. Burton thrived in this unorthodox environment, but Hasluck suffered a great deal of disquiet".[43]

Despite having hardly seen his family in months and

missing them, at the conclusion of the San Francisco Conference, Hasluck joined the Evatt team in a leisurely sea trip home even while he would have preferred to fly. Then, with just a few days to join Alexandra and the boys in Perth, Hasluck was sent back to London as Australia's representative on the executive committee of the Preparatory Commission in advance of the convening of the first session of the United Nations.

As a sort of pig in the middle, Hasluck's time in London was complicated by a rift between Evatt and Australia's High Commissioner in London, Stanley Melbourne Bruce. Evatt, in his suspicious way, would not allow Hasluck to involve Bruce in Hasluck's work. Defying this order, Hasluck told Bruce that he would send all his communications with Evatt through Australia House. Bruce gave Hasluck his full support.[44]

Before the end of Hasluck's stint in London, he was advised that he was to go to New York as Australia's delegate to the UN Security Council. This meant staying in London until March 1946 before moving to New York. Alix and the boys joined him there in May – after a journey across the US plagued by missing train carriages, heat in unairconditioned railway carriages and the general sparseness of post war conditions. Writing to her mother from New York as they settled in, Alix captured the highs and lows:

> I have stepped right from a four and a half day train journey that was a nightmare of discomfort, right into the midst of the most fantastic experience, dining nightly with millionaires and the great of the earth ... how tired I was the next two days, Paul

being wearing. … he was on the eve of making an attack on Russia for walking out of the Security Council. Evatt wouldn't give him any directions & he was left to decide to do it himself. He did it the next Wednesday and hit the headlines. At present he is the man of the moment.[45]

He may have been the man of the moment but, as he has recorded, "Evatt was not pleased". Evatt had not allowed Hasluck the title of ambassador to the Security Council preferring to keep that for himself. If, then, Hasluck was getting such recognition, it would not do. "He told me," wrote Hasluck, "I was getting too much publicity and not giving enough credit to him …The Security Council had really meant him to be chairman not me".[46] As Australia's representative, Hasluck had chaired the sub-committee which had been designated to investigate the Russian dispute with Iran.

In *Diplomatic Witness*, Hasluck sketches a cameo that reveals much of the self-importance and sham pomp of Evatt's demeanour. Prior to arriving in London, Evatt had openly expressed his view that Churchill was "getting away with too much" and "someone had to stand up to him". The impression given was that Evatt would be the one to do it. Evatt and Deputy PM Frank Forde, with advisers, met with Churchill in the War Cabinet room at No 10 while they were in London in April 1945. As they were seated around the table, Churchill called on various ministers by name to speak and then would stop them abruptly with "That'll do" when he'd heard enough. Eden followed by Cranborne got their "That'll do". At the end of the meeting, as Australia's Forde was expressing his appreciation for the meeting, Evatt pulled Forde's sleeve as if he had something to say. So, Forde noted to the assembled that Dr Evatt had something to add. Hasluck described what happened:

> Evatt squared himself at the table eagerly. Churchill swung slowly in his chair. His jaw stuck out and his baby-blue eyes stared unwinkingly at Evatt. He leaned forward. "Oh, Doctor Evatt would like to say something," he growled slowly. He leaned further forward, head out-thrust. "And what exactly does Doctor Evatt propose to say?" It was a direct challenge. Evatt wilted. He stammered uncertainly a few sentences to the effect he supported what the Deputy Prime Minister of Australia had said. Churchill heard him, still staring intensely and, after pausing a while to accentuate Evatt's confusion, called on the Prime Minister of New Zealand to address us.[47]

In early 1947, John Burton was appointed head of the department of External Affairs. After careful consideration of his future, which he did not want to be either as a UN official or officer of the department, Hasluck advised Evatt he would resign from April that year. He added that the lease on the family's New York Bronxville house was due to expire around that time. Hasluck records in *Diplomatic Witness* the displeasure Evatt showed on hearing this, a reaction which darted from wanting to sack Hasluck to wanting him to stay longer. Eventually, Hasluck got his way. In a letter to his departmental colleague Ken Bailey, Hasluck gave an account of his feelings at the time among which was that he feared the appointment of Burton would endanger the department's impartiality and integrity when carrying out its function of presenting and analysing facts. Under Burton's style, its public servants would be "turned into the tools of ministers and corrupted by a system of favours".[48]

On 1 July, the somewhat relieved and relaxed Haslucks embarked on the *Port Chalmers* in New York to begin their long trip home to Perth, via the Panama Canal. In November 1944, Hasluck had accepted a commission to be one of the official war historians to write on the civil aspects of the war. He would now complete the project. Apart from that, he saw an academic life as his next move. The following year, Hasluck commenced as a Reader in History at the University of Western Australia. He was also called on to speak on international affairs by the ABC and at various adult education classes. In New York, he had done much circuit speaking with the Security Council. He also submitted for publication a quick work on his time with the Security Council which was published in August 1948 as *Workshop of Security*. He then started work on his war history which demanded a lot of travel to archives. In Canberra, he encountered resistance from Burton at External Affairs and his general editor Gavin Long had to ask Ben Chifley to intervene. Given the files, Hasluck found many documents he knew to have existed had vanished and, in general, they were in a chaotic order.[49] In 1952, *The Government and the People, 1939-1941*. (Vol I) was published to rave reviews. The second volume involved additional researchers and appeared eventually in 1970 as *The Government and the People 1942-45*.

Paul Hasluck MP

In 1949, a new electorate was created on the western side of the Swan River in Perth, taken from parts of the seat of Fremantle which had been Prime Minister John Curtin's seat. Hence the name of Curtin given it. Apart from the fact that the Haslucks lived well inside this new electorate, Paul Hasluck had become known for his addresses on international relations and foreign policy and noted for his relatively conservative outlook. At some point in early 1949, as the Liberal Party looked for a candidate for Curtin, Hasluck was approached by the General Secretary of the Liberal and Country League of Western Australia to ask if he would agree to stand as the Liberal Party's candidate for Curtin – at the time considered Labor territory.

Hasluck took up the challenge, albeit not expected to win. But he expressed a new faith in a fresh start telling *The Daily Telegraph*: "Because I believe in parliamentary democracy, Parliament appears to be a way in which one can best serve, to try to maintain what he regards as the Australian way of life." He also said that on his return to Australia, after years abroad, he found that "class war was being actively preached" and that comradeship among Australians had been "impaired".[50] Decades later, looking back, he declared that the move to parliament was one of the "turning points" in his life.[51]

Hasluck won the seat. Alix Hasluck has written that her husband made a good candidate. While he could be a difficult task master at the office, out among electors he was a different person: "He really enjoyed making contact with strangers and yarning with them, and in certain districts found that his name was already known by reason of his father's connection with people through his religion, or through historical knowledge of families from earlier days".[52]

As a new member of the federal parliament, Paul Hasluck was quite unusual. Having completed his war history, the first volume of which would be published in his second year as an MP, Hasluck's knowledge of the parliament and government was huge. He had written about many of the players still in government. At first, indeed for some years, he was no favourite of Robert Menzies even though he respected his leader very much. In an interview prior to the 50th anniversary of the founding of the Liberal Party, Hasluck told Gerard Henderson why he thought his relations with Menzies needed time to settle:

> ...in my first volume of the war history... I made a character assessment of Menzies which I think was fair and which some other people have said is accurate, but it was possibly not the picture Menzies had of himself. And that may have been one reason. ... In the beginning I think he was a bit suspicious of me ... [and] it was true of Menzies at that period. My judgement is that Menzies took to heart some very bitter lessons from his downfall in 1941 and, in his second term as Prime Minister, he became a different sort of Prime Minister resulting from the lessons he learnt. ... he was more tolerant towards people who had stupid arguments. He let them go on, he didn't try to snub them or anything like that. Whereas - I wasn't there at the time – but I gather that in his first Prime Ministership he was a bit lofty towards people of lesser brains.[53]

In parliament, Hasluck would be made a minister in just over a year. This was no doubt a recognition of his past professional life. As a minister who sat in Cabinet, it was normal for Hasluck to mix with the elite of the parliamentary team and, eventually, to witness the plotting and character assassinations of the post Menzies years. Inevitably, there would be some he found not to his liking and, as always with Paul Hasluck, he did not suffer bores gladly. Asked in the 1980s, by former Labor minister Clyde Cameron, to comment on how some of his colleagues regarded him as somewhat aloof and distant, Hasluck laughed it off saying that, for some, "I didn't like them; they didn't like me".[54]

Hasluck was to become very disillusioned with the calibre of new MPs in the years beyond the intake of 1949. However, it was the behaviour of a forty-niner (as they were known) who troubled him most as the years went on. This was William McMahon, who succeeded John Gorton as Prime Minister in March 1971. Asked by Gerard Henderson about his view of McMahon, Hasluck's response hit the mark:

> GH: You said before that on Holt's death he was totally unsuitable. I mean subsequently it became evident that he was totally unsuitable. Why did you find him unsuitable?
>
> PH: To speak succinctly, the man is a treacherous liar.
>
> GH: Well, that's true.
>
> PH: A treacherous liar.
>
> GH: But then again, it's odd, in a way, is it not, that a treacherous liar like McMahon got so far in

the Party?

PH: Oh, that's how he got there, by treachery and by lying.[55]

From the outset, as an MP, Paul Hasluck had pure aims and policy ambitions. His maiden speech was given in the House of Representatives on 1 March 1950. He noted the honour bestowed on him to be the first member for the seat of Curtin, named after a man he had known "as a colleague in journalism, and as a friend long before he entered parliament". Hasluck spoke of John Curtin in the most notable of terms for his raising the Labor Party to "the highest level of respect it has ever enjoyed in this country" as well as of Curtin's respect for parliamentary institutions and his faith in the possibility of using the parliament to obtain the best results for the whole nation".[56]

Arguing for domestic and foreign policy to be more aligned, Hasluck pointed to the need for post war adjustments to national focus saying that "when thinking of defence in Australia today, our eyes must turn westward if that policy is to be effective, and the importance of the Indian Ocean, both in our international relations and in our preparations for defence of this country, must be recognised." He finished on a unifying note acknowledging there would always be differences of approach but affirming that "the good of Australia in the sense of the whole nation shall be the supreme thought".[57]

Minister of the Crown

> Twelve years as Minister for Territories killed in me all personal ambition and deadened my political interest. Yet it gave me a range of administrative experience that exceeded by far that of any Federal ministerial colleague, for in a country of two million people I was virtually the Premier and the whole of a state Cabinet.[58]

In just over a year from taking office, the Menzies government fought a double dissolution election in the midst of challenges associated with its Communist Party Dissolution legislation. On 28 April 1951, the Menzies government was re-elected gaining a majority in the Senate. As portfolios were being handed out, there was a two week wait. Hasluck, assuming that no contact from the PM meant he would not be made a minister, took the family on a fishing holiday to Augusta. After just two days of fishing, a phone call ended the holiday and sent Hasluck to Brisbane for a meeting with Menzies who was dining with guests at a local hotel. Here he was pressured, more or less, into accepting the new portfolio of Territories with responsibility for the Northern Territory and Papua New Guinea. He would also be in Cabinet. Writing of this many years later, Hasluck recalls his feelings of irritation as he accepted the post, as if he "had been brought in reluctantly at the last minute as a tail-ender ... Why use me here when there were other things I could do better?"[59] The only positive Hasluck could see at the time was that the job would give him the chance to renew his work for the welfare of Australian Aboriginals.

From 1906, Australia had been given the responsibility

for the administration of the south eastern section of New Guinea while the Germans annexed the north eastern section as Kaiser Wilhelmsland. In World War I, Australian military forces had occupied Kaiser Wilhelmsland to prevent it being used by the Germans as a military naval base. After the Treaty of Versailles, Australia was given control of Kaiser Wilhelmsland, although the two parts of eastern New Guinea were administered separately. In 1949, Papua and New Guinea were brought together under one administration based in Port Moresby.

As Minister for Territories from early 1951, Hasluck's task was to unite historically divided native peoples brought together on a map in a UN devised territory. This geographical collective was expected to develop modern standards in an increasingly westernised global community. It was a territory of rudimentary infrastructure, under resourced, vastly damaged by war and inhabited by people who had but a basic idea (in many cases no idea) of what the West knew as "civilisation". In 1949, Australia's administrative white colonists, on the whole, still operated in the manner of colonial masters. In addition to Papua New Guinea, Hasluck was also responsible for smaller territories in Papua New Guinea's vicinity such as Nauru, Ashmore and Cartier Islands and New Norfolk.

In spite of Hasluck's initial lack of interest in the portfolio of Territories and his belief he was hardly qualified, his biographer Geoffrey Bolton saw it another way. Apart from his dogged determination to master a job and do it well, Hasluck had gained much in experience of post-colonial policy while at the UN. As Bolton put it, "It would have been hard to find any other member of parliament with superior claims. Hasluck proved to be the only minister capable of overseeing the Northern Territory on the one hand and the overseas territories such as Papua New Guinea on the other".[60] That Hasluck left his mark on Papua New Guinea as an administrator and leader is testimony to Bolton's view. Asked by Gerard Henderson how and why he stayed so long, Hasluck was realistic:

> I stayed in Territories for 12 years, and I think there's a combination of two or three reasons. One was that Menzies began to get an appreciation of the historical importance of what was happening in New Guinea and wanted me to continue doing it. He took more and more interest in what I was doing. Another reason was that because of the lack of political value in Territories, no one else wanted the portfolio. It was hard to get anyone else to take it. And I suppose, up to a stage, I was quite engrossed in the job.[61]

The task given Hasluck in his new portfolio was immense. It took months of advice and travelling to take it all in. While some 325,123 square kilometres of territory in Papua New Guinea was under some degree of administrative control, there was still some 150,245 square kilometres of extremely isolated territory untouched. The Australian administrators already in place were a mixed bunch – some professionally adept while others were time servers enjoying a colonial life.

Professor O.H.K Spate, Foundation Professor of Geography in the Research School of Pacific Studies at The Australian National University from 1951, visited Papua New Guinea in 1951 and 1953 and was appalled by the structure and quality of the local public service and its uncoordinated efforts.[62] This was confirmed by Hasluck's own recordings of his early experience. As for resources, wharves, roads, housing, schools, administrative buildings and electricity supplies, these were all in primitive condition. Then there was the overall imitation of British colonial mores where some of the white inhabitants were assisted in everything – from carrying parcels and cleaning shoes to opening car doors – by house boys. In Hasluck's view this was not the way one ruled dependent peoples. The task ahead was huge.

It would take Hasluck some years to get the settings right – or at least on track for development. Hasluck's *A Time for Building* has left a comprehensive record. Clearly though, Hasluck himself benefitted from his years in the Department of External Affairs and his understanding of the glacial movement of government and bureaucracy. Early on, he developed ideas about a "territorial service" to more closely bring professional experience to the changes needed to be made. It fell on deaf ears. Hasluck then decided to work around the road blocks of Canberra administration. In just two years, he could report the inauguration of a Legislative Council, the appointment of Brigadier (later Sir) Donald Cleland as new Administrator, fresh talent and new energy among administrative staff and increased government involvement in the sale and distribution of land so as not to disrupt native interests. For all that, the challenges presented by health and education he saw as "stupendous".[63]

Hasluck took to his ministerial duties like a man driven by his ambitions for his charges. In the case of administrations at Darwin in the Northern Territory and Port Moresby in Papua New Guinea, Hasluck as Minister "oversaw policy constantly and intervened frequently". He saw many obstacles in the bureaucratic set up and was determined to overcome them, a stickler for correct procedure. He was also one who found a written directive more forceful than an irritated conversation.[64] This often left observers and participants critical of his administrative style but, over time, it had results. The former minister in charge, Percy Spender, had issued a five-year plan that proposed all of the Papua New Guinea territories be under the administration's care by 1955. This was a target too far, but Hasluck admitted it was a way of pushing more rapid development.

In time, Hasluck pushed and created a much more indigenous political structure with the formation of the Papua New Guinea Legislative Assembly. As he had always done for Australian Aboriginals, he advocated racial equality, telling the parliament in 1954, "We have established a principle that if a native can qualify on the same level as a European, he should enter the public service on the same footing".[65] But many of his farsighted attempts to move more progressive policy were "undermined by the officials charged with implementing his policies".[66] While much was achieved in twelve years, Hasluck would look back and regret he did not accomplish more in education where entrenched native customs, especially re women, resisted change. In addition, not always satisfactory mission schools continued to absorb far more pupils than government schools.

Biographer Geoffrey Bolton traces the considerable strain

Hasluck's ministerial responsibilities and long absences placed on Alix who discovered her career as a writer as a result of being mostly sidelined by her husband's new political life. But they continued a strong bond with Alix travelling to Canberra where their sons were boarding at Canberra Grammar and in long letters they wrote to each other. As one who loved travel to foreign places, Alix also recorded many of the trips to the territories she made with her husband, trips which she saw as compensation for the long weeks of separation. Relating the ordeals of some occasions at various remote locations in Papua New Guinea, Alix described one particularly unusual embarkation for Australians making official visits:

> Taking to the flying-boat again, we set off for the island of Daru, some hundreds of miles north-east of the Cape York peninsula ... We came down on a rather choppy sea way out from a long jetty. A curious rough kind of raft made from planks mounted on two canoes was making its way towards us ... My husband embarked first, promptly putting his foot through a loose plank up to his thigh.[67]

There was no quick solution to the task ahead of Australia's administration of Papua New Guinea. Yet, Hasluck's ability to grind away at the obstacles from complacent and defeated officials on site to uninterested bureaucrats dealing with staffing and budgets in Canberra to the vested interests of some investors with links to Liberal Party MPs was just what was needed. Budgets improved, infrastructure was built, a fragile sense of nationhood unfolded. But support and enthusiasm for his work remained lacking from his party colleagues. During parliamentary debates in May and September 1959, discussing Territory estimates, Hasluck recalled that his chief supporters were Labor's Kim Beazley and Arthur Calwell. At the time, some opponents within the Liberal Party had tried to have Hasluck removed from office due his perceived hostility to "private enterprise".[68] This related to the government control of land sales in Papua New Guinea where legislation was designed to protect local residents from being victims of offshore purchases for business investment. The idea was that investment was welcome but not at the expense of native interests.

As Sir William Slim was about to leave Australia at the end of his term as Australia's Governor-General in 1960, he spoke with Hasluck in admiring terms. He noted that one matter the Menzies government had done well was the administration of Papua New Guinea. A military man, Slim acknowledged the huge task of bringing into modernity such diverse and unspoiled remote tribal peoples, saying: "Your young chaps in New Guinea have gone out where I would never have gone without a battalion and they have done on their own by sheer force of character what I could only do with troops. I don't think there has been anything like it in the modern world".[69]

Slim was referring in particular to the patrol officers who went into the remote regions to help local villages make contact with the new developments and administration. These patrol officers were gradually offered the rustic benefit of landing strips – sometimes just strips of grass tusks – where small single engine planes made precarious landings, often using river valleys to find their way. One pilot with Hasluck on board told him as they landed that his concern was not with getting down but estimating how he could take off. On many of these flights, Hasluck trusted to the instincts of such pilots more so than mechanical ingenuity.

Hasluck was keen especially that education as a basis for indigenous involvement in civic life would be spread as widely as possible. Village councils were set up with leaders emerging among native settlements. In time, these would service increasing numbers of indigenous people as part of the developing representative government institutions, initially the Legislative Council. Language could be a barrier but increasingly translators and education would bring more unity. And there were leaders aplenty given the tools. At a highland gathering Hasluck watched and listened to orators (their words translated for the English speaking Australians through at least two separate dialects) addressing the assembled people:

> The orators stood. Their magnificent voices rolled over the valleys and awakened echoes from the opposing slopes. ... the grand panorama of the highlands ... when they were satisfied that it was over and we had understood, they signalled to their people and a great roar of approval came from six thousand voices. It was more eloquent than words in any document about freedom from fear. We gave that freedom to half a million people who had not known it before.[70]

The Northern Territory and Aboriginal administration

As with the responsibility for Papua New Guinea, Hasluck began his time as minister responsible for the Northern Territory with similar problems. Darwin was in primitive condition as a centre of urban administration. Buildings, such as there were, had suffered the effects of war time damage and construction was minimal with the Territory bereft of government attention and funding. There had been ten different ministers in charge of the NT between 1932 and 1951. The previous minister – H L Anthony, Minister for the Interior, advised Hasluck the place was a "mess".[71]

In a short while, Hasluck had appointed a new administrator – Frank Wise – and would come to regard Wise's achievements in the role as a turning point in the development of the Northern Territory. It took longer to change the Director of Native Territories but with the appointment of Harry Giese, in a new position called Director of Welfare, progress began. While the federal opposition, in time, would attack Hasluck for a timid approach to government investment in the NT's development, Hasluck's period as Minister over 12 years contributed to the stability the Territory needed to begin positive steps to more self sufficiency in both its government institutions and its economic sustainability. Recruiting able officers for the administration continued to be difficult due to the remoteness of its location and lack of facilities.

As in Papua New Guinea, Hasluck pressed on, viewing the Northern Territory as in a pioneering stage, dependent on a younger generation of aspirational investors and settlers especially in farming and mining. For all of his so called "timidity", re government funding, expenditure sent from Canberra increased substantially over a decade. Alongside that, a select committee of the Northern Territory's Legislative Council was able to report, of the five years to 1963, that it was "greatly impressed with the evidence of the Territory's progress in the production of wealth from primary industries ... [which] greatly exceed[ed] any such figure for any state or community in Australia".[72]

It was in the administration of Aboriginal Australians in the Northern Territory that Hasluck looked forward to having some chance of initiating social change. The federal government had long since left the states to oversee the area of Aboriginal welfare and governance. Only in the Northern Territory did the federal government have responsibility for Indigenous Australians.

While Hasluck had long believed that the future of Australian Aboriginals lay in their education and adoption of mainstream Australian lifestyles, he did not initiate the policy of assimilation which such beliefs inevitably became. The 1937 conference of all state Aboriginal Boards and Protectors had concluded that assimilation was the best way forward. Hasluck took up that policy in his administration of the Northern Territory writing later:

> When I became Minister for Territories in the Australian Government in May 1951, I inherited both the word [assimilation] and the purpose it expressed. My contribution was to give greater precision to the idea, to bring clearer and more efficient measures to promote the purpose and

to seek fuller co-operation between the seven
governments in Australia engaged in this phase of
administration.[73]

Chief among Hasluck's impediments in reform of
conditions for Aboriginal Australians in the Northern
Territory was funding. In the early 1950s, the Menzies
Government was fighting the effects of inflation and most
submissions for programs needing funding for Australian
Aboriginals in the NT failed at the first jump due to
their being new funding and not as yet in any budget
and therefore an avoidable expense. Such was the way
the Commonwealth Department of the Treasury worked.
Aside from that, in Canberra, the NT was regarded as
the back of beyond, a wild untamed territory that did not
feature in bureaucratic minds when planning for urban
or regional development. This attitude also made finding
the right officers another hurdle. Hasluck found himself
advising departmental head Cecil Lambert to choose the
most senior officers from the ranks of the department
so that if an appointee proved inadequate, he could be
moved on more easily. He specifically said he did not
want an "expert" adding that, "experts could be hired like
bicycles".[74]

Central to Hasluck's take on assimilation was his long
held belief that the way forward for Aboriginal Australians
was raising them to become equal citizens with white
Australians. In this, Hasluck sought to abolish the notion
of racial protection for Aboriginal Australians and to have
all indigent citizens assessed as one – white and black
– under a welfare program. For Hasluck the notion of
protection was a negative that showed neither faith nor

hope in their future. While more progressive thinking in time would criticise the thinking behind assimilation, it needs to be understood in context. Kim Beazley (senior) reminded readers in his memoir how, in 1958, it was one of his Labor colleagues, Gordon Bryant, who spoke highly of Hasluck in the House of Representatives over his achievements for Australian Aboriginals saying: "I pay tribute to the Minister for Territories who, in spite of his conservatism, had done probably one of the best jobs for Aboriginal people than anyone in Australia has done".[75]

To abandon racial discrimination, the Northern Territory legislated in 1953 for a Welfare Branch to replace the Native Affairs Branch. The problem, however, was in the lack of a proper census count of the Aboriginal population. In time, the legislation became confined to Aboriginal people. Those under the Administrator's wings – black or white – had no citizenship rights and were "wards" until they succeeded in an appeal against the classification or were released by the Administrator. Over years, apart from the failure of the Welfare Branch to overcome Aboriginal disadvantage, Hasluck would fight the NT administration's obstruction with regard to job training and apprenticeships for young Aboriginal people and for the right to have part of their ward wages paid to them directly. The Minister had high hopes but society – big and small – would take a lot longer to adjust to Hasluck's vision.

As Frank Stevens has recorded in *Black Australia*, the Northern Territory's Employment Advisory Board did not gazette the increase in Aboriginal wages until 1959 – in spite of Hasluck's ambitions. When, finally, Aboriginal wages were determined for the cattle industry they were far below that of whites and in some cases less than in earlier years. Stevens argues that, for all the intention to release Aboriginal employees and those dependent on government, the 1950s was "anything but a period during which their status was being raised to 'help them share with us the opportunities that are available in their own native land'".[76]

Speaking in parliament on 18 October 1951, Hasluck made clear his expectations of assimilation:

> Assimilation means, in practical terms, that, in the course of time, it is expected that all persons of Aboriginal blood or mixed blood in Australia will live as do white Australians. The acceptance of this policy governs all other aspects of native affairs administration. ... Another alternative is segregation ... segregation could take place in settlements and missions solely occupied by natives. The objection to this policy is that, if it succeeds, we shall build up in Australia an ever-increasing body of people who belong to a separate caste, and who live in Australia but are not members of the Australian community. We shall create a series of minority groups who live in little bits of territory of their own.[77]

Decades later, the centralised policy of assimilation would become rejected and seen as tragically misguided because it ushered in a policy of the removal of half caste children from (mostly) their Aboriginal mothers. In many cases, single mothers willingly gave their offspring to the state especially when poverty and the difficulties of single parenting arose. This was true also of white parents handing over children to orphanages such as those run by the Sisters of St Joseph – men left with children after the death of a wife for example.

But there was also the separation trauma, especially with so many half caste Aboriginal children in indigent circumstances. Indigenous Australians' leader Lowitja O'Donoghue, was handed over to missionaries, along with most of her siblings, by her father Tom. He worked in the cattle industry and overruled his Aboriginal wife sending the children away. In the debates over what was termed the "stolen generations" decades later, media figure Andrew Bolt accused O'Donoghue of falsifying her record saying she was not stolen. O'Donoghue admitted she was "removed" not stolen, but that her mother had only given "uninformed consent"'.[78]

There were others, not unlike O'Donoghue, who valued the education and chance of a successful life they were given by the separation from their often single parents. Geelong AFL football great Polly Farmer told his biographer Steve Hawke that he was fortunate to be given up to Sister Kate's orphanage by his single mother who could not support him.[79] This was also what he told Tony Boti who wrote in Farmer's obituary: "Unlike the experience of others placed in various institutions for Aboriginal children, Farmer was grateful for his time at Sister Kate's and believed it provided him with a good start in life".[80] Ironically, at the expense of family ties and loss of their cultural background, assimilation at that time brought hundreds of Aboriginal children into mainstream Australian society. Many of the future leaders in the

Indigenous movements to come developed their advocacy skills as removed or stolen children, or as the sons and daughters of removed or stolen Indigenous children.

As Geoffrey Bolton writes: "Assimilation was not intended as cultural genocide. Hasluck, in common with most observers at that time, believed that traditional Aboriginal society, a hunter-gatherer regime, nomadic within understood boundaries, was in irreversible decline. … Assimilation was the consequence not the cause of these changes".[81] Unlike the eugenic policies of the 1930s, however, Hasluck was not concerned with racial demise but with the welfare of the children who were rejected not only by white society but also in many places by full blooded Aboriginal communities.

It was the economic development of the Northern Territory which often most concerned Hasluck. Industries developing in mining and agriculture would take the territory closer to more self sufficiency. But land being taken for such industries also put pressure on what remained of Aboriginal land rights. In this, Hasluck refused to allow Aboriginal reserves to be opened up for pastoral leases even if those reserves had no economic benefit to their Aboriginal wanderers – the land had more meaning to them than simply employment. Hasluck understood the reserves' importance to Aboriginal identity and sentiment. Where Aboriginal land became important to the mining industry, Hasluck was the first minister, Commonwealth or state, to insist that Aboriginal Australians should share the benefits of mineral development in the territory.[82]

While the policy of assimilation would govern Indigenous policy in the 1950s and into the 1960s, it was often debated. Anthropologist Professor A P Elkin, in time, preferred the concept of integration which accepted the need for Aboriginal Australians not only to adapt to the mores of white Australians but also allow them to retain contact with their native symbols and history. Hasluck took a long view himself, considering how Britain had developed from centuries of invading peoples so that the result was a blend of many parts. Invasion, settlement and peoples' rights came at much expense, but it could work over time. Along the way, Hasluck might be accused of too hopeful a view of outcomes. For example, the adoption of equal pay for Aboriginal stockmen had the unintended consequences of most of them losing their jobs. The result was that many Aboriginal families were ejected from cattle stations where their lives had been maintained for so long with homes and benefits and connection to their spiritual lands. They inevitably ended up on social service payments and pensions and with no need to seek employment. The era of "sit-down" money began.

Equality for Aboriginal Australians took a big step in 1962 when the Menzies Government legislated to give Aboriginal Australians the option to enrol and vote in federal elections. This was closely followed that same year in Western Australia and the Northern Territory when Aboriginal people were given the vote in the elections of Western Australia and the Northern Territory. Hasluck had achieved his long held wish for Aboriginal Australians under his watch.

In the House, Hasluck continued defending assimilation as a preferred policy and was often opposed by Kim Beazley (senior), another Western Australian but a Labor MP. It was, then, a measure of Hasluck's integrity when

Kim Beazley presented an Aboriginal petition against the lack of consultation in the acquisition of Yirrkala mission land for a bauxite mine. Beazley presented the petition arguing that Aboriginal reserves meant nothing if they were so easily given up for commercial interests. Beazley wrote of how "To my astonishment Hasluck … rose immediately and said 'The Government readily accepts the proposal'." Beazley later wrote that Hasluck's action, in accepting an opposition proposal and acting to sort it out, was unique and something he had never seen in 30 years of his parliamentary experience. He went on to declare that "Hasluck was that rare politician who can genuinely be called a statesman".[83]

Reflecting on developments for Indigenous Australians in 1988, Hasluck saw what he called "abject despair" replaced by "hope or intention about the future". He added, "Even the fact of the present-day protest is in itself a sign that Aboriginals have an expectation of better times ahead." Looking back, he also acknowledged that his push for Indigenous Australians to have the right to vote was essential to getting politicians to take notice of them and to work for their welfare. But he warned, "I question the wisdom of any policy or any administrative measures that separate Aboriginals from other Australians and I doubt whether in the long run it will serve the interests of the Aboriginals".[84] In 2023, the overwhelming rejection of such a separation in the constitutional referendum proposal, known as "the Voice", by the Australian electorate and in debates beforehand that bitterly divided Australians, is a recognition that this advice of Sir Paul Hasluck, a former Governor-General of Australia, should be taken seriously.

The grit of External Affairs

Hasluck would complete his parliamentary years as Minister of External Affairs – the top job for which he once was a close adviser when its minister was Bert Evatt. How the wheels had turned. Following the November 1963 federal election, Menzies finally moved Hasluck from Territories. He was given instead the portfolio of Defence. But that would last just a few months. In April 1964, Sir Owen Dixon retired as Chief Justice and Garfield Barwick was appointed in his place leaving the portfolio of External Affairs vacant. Menzies then accepted that Hasluck should at long last be given the ministry he was best qualified for.

External Affairs in the 1940s when Hasluck had served was a portfolio experiencing a global war that then became a period of re-establishment of world order and new visions for peace. In this, Hasluck had a seat at the table establishing the United Nations. By 1964, Australia's focus was closer to home as the newly emerging nations of South-east Asia shook off their colonial governments. It was also an era that lived in the shadow of war while hoping that engagement and negotiation would stabilise regional conflict. But it was also a time of increasing local uprisings where communist insurgents sought to take over established administrations behind the cry of independence and freedom from colonial rulers.

In Malaya, communist insurgents fought Commonwealth and Malayan forces from 1949 to 1960 in what became known as the Malayan Emergency. Australia sent forces in support of the Malayan and Commonwealth forces. In Korea, in 1950, the United Nations authorised military engagement against North Korea (backed by Communist China) after North Korea invaded South Korea. Australia joined the UN forces along with some 21 other countries. The war ended in the division of the Korean peninsular rather than a peace treaty. In Indonesia, President Sukarno had been the leader of the Indonesian nationalists who wrested government from the Netherlands in 1949. He eventually established an authoritarian hold over the country with sympathetic links to the Soviet Union while speaking well of China and Marxism in general. In 1962, Sukarno secured control of Dutch West Irian and in 1963 Indonesia stirred trouble over the establishment of the Federation of Malaysia resulting in what came to be known as the *Konfrontasi* (Confrontation).

For Australia, such developments in Indonesia were of concern. While Sukarno professed not to be a communist, he told the US Ambassador, in March 1958, "that he had seen in Communist China such tremendous economic advances that he believed Communist Chinese methods held lessons for Indonesia". [85] Indonesia's conflict with Malaysia and subsequent territorial disputes caused concern with the Australian government that Papua New Guinea could be next. Menzies' overriding concern was to keep the US onside recognising its support could well be needed in confronting Indonesia. As Hasluck took over External Affairs, Indonesia was of greater concern than the growing conflict in Vietnam, but it would be Vietnam which would test the Menzies government and its External Affairs minister.

On 23 March 1965, almost a year since becoming External Affairs Minister, Hasluck made his first significant address to parliament as minister. The address analysed the government's view of the post war stage where nuclear power had diminished large conflict but where the rise of communist agitation had increased smaller conflicts, where "troubles which might seem local and trivial at first sight have been promoted or expanded as the result of influences controlled by great powers".[86] Hasluck then moved to the situation in Vietnam which he said was not a local rebellion but an extension of "the methods and doctrines of Communist guerrilla warfare first evolved in China and then successfully used in North Vietnam". Thus, as the US and Australia saw it, the South Vietnamese were dealing with "a large-scale directed campaign of assassination and terrorism ... from the outside". From this he argued that the United States could not withdraw from Vietnam "without considering the world wide impact of such a withdrawal on the broader strategies of world politics".

As Peter Edwards has commented, the speech did not generate much interest in the House. But it did lead to Labor opponents admitting they valued the US presence in South-east Asia. Labor leader Arthur Calwell warned that the war must not be widened for fear that the US would be humiliated by defeat.[87] Kim Beazley went further suggesting those who called for the US to leave were in fact calling for the US to surrender.[88]

For all that, the speech did not go down well with the press where more specifics were needed as hearsay grew that Australia could become more involved in Vietnam on the ground. The speech was called cold and intellectual but, as historian Peter Edwards has demonstrated, "Hasluck could not tell them that the Australian Government was once again in its familiar position of uncertainty about the future of United States policy". Over some weeks, Cabinet debated Australia's position on Vietnam with Paul Hasluck and William McMahon arguing for a more reserved decision only to be gradually outvoted by Menzies and McEwen and members of the Cabinet committee of Foreign Affairs and Defence (FAD). On 29 April, Robert Menzies announced that Australia would be sending a battalion to join forces supporting the South in Vietnam.[89]

The decision to send an Australian battalion to Vietnam would change the atmospherics around the debate over the war in Australia. In November 1964, the Menzies Government had reintroduced the conscription of young men to provide greater numbers for the Australian Army. The concern at the time was the Confrontation conflict in Malaysia and the increasing involvement of Indonesia. With the commitment of an Australian battalion to Vietnam in April 1965, the realities of conscription began to hit home as 20-year-olds, chosen by ballot, could now be sent off to combat after preliminary training. While the Australian public was initially supportive of the move, protests from those opposed to the commitment started to grow. A statement by the prime minister while in London in June that Australia was at war sparked questions from Opposition leader Calwell over lack of information and the fact that parliament had not been informed of such a state of war. Menzies muted his stance on return and hinted he was thinking of his retirement.[90] Across the world heads of government argued the best way forward was seeking co-operation in negotiation for peace with the North Vietnamese while the North Vietnamese communist leaders remained obdurate that they were not open to negotiation.

One of the consistent arguments from the opponents of Australia's Vietnam commitment was that Australia was a lackey of the US and merely following the larger power rather than seeking Australia's best interests. For all that, the anti-war movements in Australia also followed the US in their opposition to Australia's Vietnam commitment. What happened in the US soon happened in Australia. Significantly, in 1965, groups in Australian universities began to hold what were called "teach-ins". A phenomenon copied from the US. A teach-in would call a large audience of students and others to assemble in a university venue to listen to the speeches of public leaders arguing both for and against the war.

On 25 June, the University of Queensland held Australia's first teach-in sponsored by the university's Labor Club. On 23 July 1965, some 700-800 people, mostly students, on a cold Canberra night at the Australian National University, sat until 3.30am listening to 16 speakers. Organised by the Professor of Far Eastern history, C.P. Fitzgerald, the gathering brought into public prominence academics and political activists as opponents of the government. The meeting was robust and drew audience cheers and interruptions. A new era of political protest was underway. And a new era of government defence of its policies likewise.

Paul Hasluck accepted an invitation to speak at the next teach-in, held at Monash University on 29 July. It was organised by a diverse group of university political clubs and had eight speakers. It was also filmed for television and widely reported in the daily newspapers. An estimated 2000 students and others attended. Perhaps

Hasluck was not aware of the political ferment of the growing resistance to Australia's Vietnam commitment or perhaps he thought a teach-in was just another forum for university style lectures. His performance suggested he expected a reasonable audience ready to hear the facts as he saw them. But teach-ins called for the demagoguery of impassioned believers.

Hasluck's speech, lasting an hour, did not resonate. And he later complained about interjections. As a university student, commentator Gerard Henderson was present at the Monash teach-in and heard Hasluck speak. As he put it, he was looking forward to hearing a strong case for the government's involvement in Vietnam. Instead, he was disappointed, recalling:

> Hasluck had the information that North Vietnam was controlling the Communist Viet Cong in South Vietnam and its political arm the National Liberation Front. But he did not make the point and delivered a turgid speech without a clear and unequivocal message. It was too focused on history and did not convey the hard points in defence of Australia's commitment to South Vietnam in support of United States forces. Moreover, Hasluck lacked confidence and showed scant ability to handle interjections. He was no polemicist and looked out of place before a university audience. The only minister capable of debating the likes of Cairns was Malcolm Fraser – he addressed the second Monash teach-in when Minister for Army in October 1967 and performed very well. I also attended this function.[91]

The Australian, reporting the event in its "News Look"

section, concluded that Hasluck had "fared badly against speakers like Dr J.F. Cairns and Professor W. Macmahon Ball" before a "sceptical audience". The paper added that "the Australian Government, like the United States Government ... has been forced to recognise that the universities constitute the influential centre for criticism and critical discussion of its policies in Vietnam".[92] At this time, the Australian public supported the government's stand on Vietnam. Opposition to the war, both in the US and within Australia, however, was rapidly morphing into a full blown, pro-Communist campaign where its spokesmen pushed the argument that the war in Vietnam was a revolt in the south against a corrupt local government, an uprising from within the south over economic conditions and a push for freedom.[93]

While Hasluck had outlined historical and political contexts and the government's view of the importance of supporting a non-communist government against a Communist insurgency moving south and supported by China, Cairns had thrown the debate to more emotive areas saying the government was relying on "suspicion and fear" when there was no evidence of a downward thrust from China. He denied the Vietcong fighting in the south were being supplied by North Vietnam but by people in the South. He called for more analysis of both the political and economic situation in the war and only then could there be negotiations.[94] The fact that, as in much of the political debate, most of Cairns' argument would in time be shown to be false was not important. Emotion carried the day. Peter Edwards came to the conclusion from the documents of the event that:

> Dr Cairns' performance at the Monash teach-in,
> and his willingness similarly to address large and
> small audiences around the country, did much
> to propel him towards becoming the unofficial
> national leader of the anti-war movement. By
> contrast, Hasluck spoke "ponderously" and was
> visibly affected by interjections from a hostile
> section of the audience.[95]

The rise of the new left and the continuing strength of
the protests at Australia's involvement in the Vietnam
War, were not only beyond anything Hasluck had ever
confronted but, increasingly, would be beyond the ability
of the Menzies/Holt/Gorton/McMahon governments
to counter. In December 1965, on his return from a
successful tour of Southeast Asia, Hasluck refused to
do an Australian press conference and was confronted
by two reporters outside his office asking him why.
In response, Hasluck denied he had ever promised a
Canberra press conference and angrily "slammed his door
in the reporters' faces".[96] While Hasluck was an adept
diplomat as External Affairs minister engaging widely at
the leadership level especially in greater involvement with
the countries of Southeast Asia, the grind of the Vietnam
War protests, and journalists' zest for stories on the war,
left him looking aloof and unwilling to match the anti-war
arguments in the public domain.

Almost, not quite, Prime Minister

With Sir Robert Menzies' retirement as prime minister
on 20 January 1966, Harold Holt assumed the Liberal
leadership promoting a more modern image as prime

minister after such a long era of post war Australia and the Menzies tradition. The change of leadership refreshed Liberal popularity. At the 26 November 1966 federal election, Holt secured a landslide winning 82 seats to Labor's 41 seats. There was no Senate election. Labor's leader, the older and worn Arthur Calwell, did not go well on television against his younger opponent. Labor deputy leader Gough Whitlam would replace Calwell early in 1967.

Hasluck sensed a change of mood in party ranks with an influx of new members and a leader who was matched with an upmarket wife Zara renowned for her expertise in design and her Melbourne Toorak ambience. In May 1967, Australians voted in a referendum by a national majority of more than 90 per cent to amend Section 51 (xxvi) of the Constitution to empower the Commonwealth so that the Commonwealth would prevail over State legislation where State legislation, with respect to Aboriginal Australians, was inconsistent with Commonwealth legislation. The referendum question also deleted Section 127 of the Constitution which stated that "in reckoning the numbers of people of the Commonwealth, or of a State or other part of the Commonwealth, aboriginal natives shall not be counted".

All of this vindicated Hasluck's long argued case for equality of Aboriginal Australians as Australian citizens. However, Hasluck was not consulted or included in the decision by Holt, in the wake of the referendum result, to set up a new three-man council – the Council of Aboriginal Affairs (CAA) – which would be headed by Reserve Bank Governor Herbert Cole ("Nugget") Coombs, to identify the problems and establish communication with Aboriginal groups. The CAA was to report to the Prime Minister, not to the Minister for Territories. Hasluck saw this as a slight and an indication that his view of assimilation was to be overridden by a new approach that would encourage Aboriginal Australians to identify more with their traditional beliefs and culture. A move he believed could, in time, move towards separate development.

As one of the longest serving Liberal MPs, Hasluck's presence in the Holt years as a member of Cabinet defined him as one of the elder statesmen of the party but one who was perhaps too old-world for a generation more and more engaged in protest. When, in December 1967, Harold Holt disappeared while swimming at Cheviot Beach, Portsea, Hasluck told his wife he had no interest in replacing Holt as leader: "I did not want the prime ministership, had too little regard for many members of the Liberal Party to wish to lead them and, in any case, I had been 'rubbished' so successfully by McMahon and undermined so much by Harold himself that I doubted if anyone would want me".[97]

The white-anting of Hasluck would continue as supporters convinced Hasluck to put his name forward for the leadership which he would essentially contest against John Gorton, who would move to the lower House if he won and stand for Holt's vacant seat of Higgins. However, having put his name forward against his wife's advice, Hasluck made no approach to party colleagues for their votes while McMahon worked to have NSW colleagues vote for Gorton. Robert Menzies, writing to his daughter Heather and still in contact with seasoned Liberals, observed the following:

> Paul Hasluck is, in my opinion, possessed of the
> best brain of the whole lot; but he is now the victim
> of subtle propaganda designed to attach to the
> Gorton banner whatever sympathisers there are in
> New South Wales with Willy McMahon. The story
> is that if Hasluck wins, McMahon will be kicked
> out of Treasury. I do not believe for one moment
> that this is true and have told Paul Hasluck to take
> steps accordingly.[98]

While McMahon very much wanted the leadership himself, Country Party leader John McEwen had made it clear to Hasluck, Gorton and Governor-General Richard Casey that he would not coalition with the Liberals if McMahon was elected leader. Thereafter, McMahon was scratched from the ballot but did his best to see that Hasluck would not win.

In his letter to Heather, Menzies told his daughter that if Gorton won the leadership it would be a gift for new Labor leader Gough Whitlam who could say at the next election that there was no Liberal in the House of Representatives – the House from which a parliamentary leader is constitutionally elected – who might be leader. Hasluck ignored Menzies' warning that he should counter McMahon's lies and, while the vote was close, Gorton won. As it turned out, the Gorton-led Coalition barely scraped home at the 25 October 1969 federal election. Gorton would be toppled as leader in March 1971 leaving McMahon to gain the prize he had so long sought.

In the lead up to the 1967 leadership ballot, media interest in the contenders had sought to flesh out the winning characteristics of each man – there were four in the contest: John Gorton, Paul Hasluck, Billy Snedden and Leslie Bury. As the votes were counted at the party room meeting, just Hasluck and Gorton were left to battle it out. One of the questions Hasluck repeatedly was asked by reporters before the vote concerned the question of his reputation as an "intellectual" as if to suggest his demeanour was that of a staid professor not a leader of a government. It was noted that Hasluck had written the civil history of Australia's years in World War II and so on. He was forced to state that he was not a conservative in "the stuffy sense of the term".[99]

Following the vote to elect Gorton as leader, Hasluck recorded his observations in a long letter to Robert Menzies and in a "note" written two weeks after the ballot reflecting on the way he, by then, realised how the leadership contest had unfolded. These can be found in his published collection edited by his son Nicholas Hasluck - *The Chance of Politics.* To Menzies, he wrote of how naïve he had been not to have realised what scheming had preceded the election of Gorton. Gorton had won, Hasluck realised, by gathering the votes of what Hasluck called "three streams" (Gorton supporters plus McMahon anti-Hasluck white-anters) while he had only one. He could by then recognise that McMahon had been working in the shadows against Holt even before his death since the Holt government had been in serious trouble and sliding in popularity rapidly after Holt's easy victory in 1966.

Hasluck's "note" begins with the words: "I have been living in a state of political innocence" and goes on to describe how he had discovered that Gorton had been plotting a leadership challenge to Holt backed by McMahon. Reassessing a conversation Hasluck had had with Gorton on that fateful Sunday evening, Hasluck realised Gorton had been considering a move to the lower house well before Holt's disappearance. As Hasluck put it:

> I am informed that the thinking had advanced to a stage where Holt himself had become aware that a movement linking Gorton and [Billy] Wentworth was on foot and that some prospecting had been done into the possibility that Kent Hughes might be induced to retire from Chisholm to open the way for Gorton to switch from the Senate to the House of Representatives. This was resented by Kent Hughes... on the night of Holt's disappearance, in my own conversation with Gorton, it is apparent that the idea of switching from the Senate to House and seeking the leadership was not novel to him.[100]

The Queen's man Down Under

On Tuesday 11 February 1969, Australians opened their newspapers to read that Paul Hasluck would become Australia's next Governor-General on Sir Richard Casey's retirement at the end of April. At 63, Hasluck had accepted Gorton's invitation to serve in this distinguished role after serious consideration of his waning interest in parliamentary politics and his increasing age. Writing to Robert Menzies about his decision, he refuted suggestions he was being "kicked upstairs" saying: "The ultimate decision was my own, and it was made after a long and friendly discussion of the whole situation with John

Gorton. ... the higher appointment had to be filled, and both of us felt that at this particular juncture it had to be filled by an Australian, that the person appointed would have to have the sensitivity for Australian politics and at least some appreciation of the Constitutional position".[101]

While some like Menzies were concerned at the appointment of a serving MP to the job, most welcomed the news with Evan Williams at *The Sydney Morning Herald* writing:

> In no one else... would the appointment of an active politician as Governor-General seem less objectionable. In his 20 years as a Minister (he has never really been a backbencher at all) he has shown such monarchical indifference to the skirmishing and jockeying of politics that it seems almost insulting to call him a politician at all.[102]

Alix Hasluck had come around to the move after being assured she would have time each day for her own pursuits. In fact, as the time wore on in the job, she would find that she and Paul barely saw one another privately, such was the schedule of work Hasluck undertook and the fact that she found her husband in the job to be "very withdrawn".[103] As always, her husband had thrown himself into the work with a passion. They would spend a few weeks in February and March before the induction as ordinary Australians while Hasluck completed his second volume of *The Government and The People*, after which they spent some ten days in England in April where her husband received the honours due to his office – a Knight Grand Commander of the Order of St Michael and St George and a Knight of the Order of St John of Jerusalem.

Published a decade after taking up the Governor-General role, Paul Hasluck's *The Office of Governor-General* outlines the scrupulous standards Hasluck saw as befitting any Governor-General and his/her functions. The scrupulous public servant of his years in External Affairs now met the rigorous requirements of constitutional process and unique position as representative of the monarch of Australia. In spite of being, as Alix Hasluck related it, "rabid" at the rise of William McMahon to prime minister in March 1971, Hasluck would record in this publication: "It was my own happy experience to have enjoyed a relationship of trust and confidence with each of three successive prime ministers".[104] And, in spite of how the general public saw a Governor-General from ceremonial and official functions, Hasluck found that his experience of the role meant he spent a lot of time at his desk reading the mountain of papers that came across it.[105]

Granted the Governor-General role did not involve so much travel as it does some half a century on, Hasluck did spend a lot of time writing and researching his speeches. A young Peter Cosgrove who would, decades later, himself be Australia's Governor-General, was the Army's Aide-de-Camp from November 1971 to November 1972 at Government House. He looked back, in an interview for The Sydney Institute, on his days with Hasluck and how he found the man who was his boss:

> I heard him give numerous speeches. He would write them all; in those days there wasn't anything like a speechwriter. He'd sit down and away he'd go. ... The speeches he gave were masterpieces. I'd sit in the audience and they were so thoughtful. But he was shy; he was not naturally gregarious.

When he interacted with a room full of people, you could see that he was holding back a bit, he wasn't exuberant. But boy, did he have gravitas. And because he'd been a senior politician, when MPs came Paul would know what was going through their minds.[106]

A year out from the end of his five-year term, Hasluck advised Whitlam that, for personal reasons, he would retire from the role in 1974. Whitlam had wanted the Haslucks to extend their term for another two years, but Hasluck explained that his wife's deteriorating hip and the pain she had experienced for some time meant that she wished to seek surgery in Perth and was unsure how it might affect her future. In addition, on 5 June, they had received news that their elder son Rollo had collapsed and died while on a trip with friends in Singapore. He had contracted an infection and died of myocardial infarction, aged just 34.[107] In time, Alix's operation would be successful and they had reservations about Hasluck's successor John Kerr when it was realised his wife was an invalid undergoing treatment for cancer. But, by then, John Kerr had accepted the appointment. All of which leaves open a huge hypothetical – would there have been no dismissal of the Whitlam Government in November 1975 had Hasluck stayed on?

In Hasluck's *The Office of Governor-General*, there are clues as to how he believed a Governor-General could respond to the events leading up to something like the dismissal of the Whitlam Government by John Kerr. But there are few clues as to what Hasluck might have done himself when presented with the crisis that led to the dismissal. Ever the process perfectionist, Hasluck believed that, while running nothing as part of the government, "[the Governor-General] occupies a position where he can help ensure that those who conduct the affairs of the nation do so strictly in accordance with the Constitution and the laws of the Commonwealth and with due regard to the public interest". Moreover in "abnormal times", while the Governor-General could not over-rule elected representatives, he believed that the Governor-General could "check" the elected representatives in extreme situations by "forcing a crisis".[108]

Hasluck always refused to offer an opinion on John Kerr's decision on 11 November 1975 that removed Whitlam as Prime Minister and replaced him with opposition leader Malcolm Fraser. This came after the Opposition blocked supply and Whitlam wanted to govern without supply. However, in his "Charteris Memo", written around the time of John Kerr's retirement as Governor-General in August 1977 after a long discussion with Sir Martin Charteris on 1 August 1977 at Buckingham Palace, he gave reasons to believe he saw some responsibility on Kerr's part for what had happened leading up to 11 November 1975. At the time, there were concerns at the Palace that Kerr would publish a memoir after his retirement and the Palace wanted to be sure that Kerr would abide by the advice that all the communications between the Queen and the Governor-General over the dismissal of the Whitlam Government were the Queen's property and not for publication. Hasluck opined to Charteris that he believed Kerr would "know what was discreet and proper" and that he would not wish "to appear to act dishonourably".[109]

Commenting further on the actual dismissal, Charteris argued that the Palace believed Kerr had acted judicially and not politically, to which Hasluck responded that in his view Kerr had acted politically in order to produce a situation where he could act judicially. There followed a conversation where both considered whether Whitlam may have thought Kerr would be his puppet while it was also clear that Whitlam had had a poor opinion of Kerr which only made the chance of the Prime Minister listening to Kerr's advice less reliable. Then Hasluck commented on how, in his belief, he thought Kerr had failed to pay close attention to the developing crisis from the "loans affair". Had he developed a closer relationship with his prime minister there might never had been a crisis.

This, of course, cannot be proven as it is mere opinion, even speculation, on the part of Hasluck whose dealings with Whitlam were much warmer than Kerr's. Moreover, Hasluck never had to deal with Whitlam at a time of political brinkmanship – a time when two monumental egos in Whitlam and Fraser were tussling for control. Hasluck also said he believed the Queen could not have dismissed Kerr without a formal submission in writing. This would have delayed proceedings to the extent it might have given Whitlam time to become more level headed. Even so, this would not have prevented a crisis. Supply would have run out, the government would have been in turmoil. And, in the end no doubt, the Queen would still have had to act on prime ministerial advice to sack the Governor-General.

It is clear from the record of the conversation between Sir Martin Charteris and Sir Paul Hasluck that the Palace viewed Hasluck's vice-regal contribution highly. This service was eventually honoured accordingly when, in April 1979, Hasluck was advised he would be made one of 24 Knights of the Garter.

Paul the Poet

It was while he was Governor-General that Paul Hasluck the poet emerged into a greater glare in the public spotlight. He had published a small collection of poetry dedicated to Alix in 1939 called *Into the Desert*. But it was his *Collected Verse* published in 1969 that brought attention to the now well known Australian as a poet. Geoffrey Lehmann reviewing the collection wrote:

> One feels with Hasluck's poetry that it is the product of the whole man, he has put all of himself into it. The poetry is passionate, lyrical, acerbic, visionary, and at times despairing. The quality that is behind all of this may be summed up by that untranslatable Latin word "virtus". Hasluck is concerned with standards and the quality of life in Australia.[110]

In his Foreword to the Collection, Hasluck gave his reasons for the late publication of poems written, mostly, over years in public life, saying, "In Australia, a politician is considered to be incapable of being a poet and his writing of verse is turned into a joke by journalists, while, on the other hand, a poet is considered to be incapable of handling any aspect of public affairs". He went on to say that in his time he had found poets he came to know as not lacking in "political guile or living in a cloud land far above political intrigue". He also wondered why "a man who uses words only for political purposes – including the yelling of an interjection such as "Sit down mug!" – is considered to have shown talents more worthy of respect than the writing of a sonnet".[111]

Indeed, Hasluck's poetry opened up many glimpses of the man himself. For Bruce Bennett, a professor of English Literature and fellow West Australian, "Hasluck's interests were broad and inclusive, and often surprising … Moreover, like many writers before him, he used his writing to experiment with different selves and ways of seeing the world".[112] Whether the natural world around him, the world that informed him from classical writers of Western civilisation and biblical themes to the weary world of professional life, Hasluck sought understanding. And revelation. Writer and arts and literature critic Rodney Hall reacted to *Collected Verse* in a wry but positive way opining: "I suppose the truth is he does it rather well. His command of technique is shaky, his subtlety of nuance is practically nil, and yet the best of these poems is utterly convincing".[113]

Following the death of his son Rollo, Hasluck produced "R" in his son's memory, capturing in 12 lines a host of feelings. The poem begins:

> You do not lie in death alone
> For some of me went with you there
> And rests forever where you rest
> And you walk with me everywhere[114]

In an email exchange in July 2025, Geoffrey Lehmann gave a brief recollection of what he saw as Hasluck's strength and weaknesses as a poet. He thought his poetry could be very accomplished with "the rhetorical style of the French nineteenth century poets" the strongest influence on his verse. One poem he found "accomplished" was "A Drunken Man on Highgate Hill" that finishes with the couplet:

> Lord of all harmony, he grunts his raucous bars
>
> Where street lamps blaze far brighter than the stars

For all that, Lehmann wrote that he regarded Hasluck's poetry as "conventional". In his *Bulletin* review, Lehmann singled out "At Wyndham" for its "keen sense of the Australian continent" – a feature of many Hasluck poems:

> The muddy tide streams up the gulf
>
> Behind the iron-roof town
>
> Mangroves, hot marsh, gaunt jelly piles
>
> Are slowly sinking down.

He noted that "Suburban Night", was "tightened by the surprise of the last line". And he found "pathos and accurate observation" in the lines:

> Sleep. Flesh renewing,
>
> Brain sloughing dry despair.
>
> On wardrobe, chair and rail discarded clothes
>
> Pattern mortality.
>
> Empty shirt ludicrous, cold the looped brassiere
>
> Bulged by relapsing breasts

Lehmann concluded his review on a positive note: "Throughout his work there is a strong sense of the man, deeply concerned with standards and the conflicts of twentieth century life. There is too much variety in the book for one to regard Hasluck as a conservative. He remains very much his own man, both scrupulous and passionate". This was also evident in a long piece written for *The Age* by Hasluck in 1979 where he not only reflected on his concern about Australians' growing and shallow consumerism but also Australian society's divisions into sectional voices and its lack of coherence around a genuine "shared vision".[115]

Hasluck filled his retirement life with those many publications, mentioned above, that recorded his various experiences of professional life. These have more than supported this brief history and evaluation of one of Australia's most distinguished public figures. He was an active speaker at events into the late 1980s. He wrote, on one occasion, that he believed that Australia would not be fully civilised "until some men will talk as naturally and as knowledgeably about poetry as most men talk about golf and the stock market".[116] This says more about Hasluck's uniqueness than it does about Australia's level of civility.

Hasluck's friend, publisher Peter Ryan, spent many hours with him both when, as Governor-General and beyond, Hasluck was publishing his later works. The two men struck up a friendship and would spend days and nights yarning before fires at their respective bush retreats. Ryan was also responsible for his Rainy Creek Press issue of Hasluck's small volume of poetry *Crude Impieties*. The picture of Hasluck that Ryan draws in his publication *Brief Lives* is of a man widely read and full of enriched conversation. But it also captures Hasluck's humble wish for ordinariness, for the ability to retreat from public recognition and just enjoy the simple pleasures of friendship and a connection with nature.

Paul Hasluck and his high-minded aspirations that could never be fully achieved left a large footprint on the nation and continent he loved. The last few lines of his poem "The Dying Explorer" are in some ways a fitting epitaph for a man who accomplished so much and yet was happiest in solitude:

> *Grudge me not this cave, this little room*
> *No chisel ring on rock metallic chime*
> *To make a record of my deeds or name*
> *Or witness who I was or why I came*
> *There's chronicle enough in undiscovered bones.*

Postscript

Sir Paul Hasluck died on 9 January 1993 at Subiaco. Alexandra Hasluck died just six months later on 18 June. The electorate of Hasluck was named after them.

Endnotes

1   Hasluck, Paul, *Crude Impieties*, Rainy Creek Press, 1991

2   Commonwealth Parliamentary Debates, (CPD), House of Representatives, 8 June 1950, p 3976

3   CPD, House of Representatives, 8 June 1950, p 3980

4   Bolton, Geoffrey, *Paul Hasluck: A Life*, University of Western Australia Publishing, 2014, p 5

5   Hasluck, Paul in *News Brief* – a publication of the Institute of Public Affairs (NSW), No 2 1988. The Institute of Public Affairs (NSW) was the predecessor of The Sydney Institute.

6   Charles, Charles, Introduction to *Paul Hasluck in Australian History*, Tom Stannage, Kay Saunders and Richard Nile, (eds,) University of Queensland Press 1999, p 2

7   Henderson, Gerard, *Menzies Child – The Liberal Party of Australia 1944-1994*, Allan & Unwin, 1994, pp 200-01

8   Richard, Nile, *Paul Hasluck in Australian History*, in Tom Stannage, Kay Saunders & Richard Nile, Preface

9   Hasluck, Paul, *Sir Robert Menzies*, Melbourne University Press, 1980, p 32. Originally delivered as the Daniel Mannix Memorial Lecture to Newman College Students at Wilson Hall, Melbourne University, June 1979.

10   Hasluck, Paul, *Mucking About An Autobiography*, Melbourne University Press 1977, p 19-26

11   Ibid., p 28

12   Bolton, Geoffrey, op cit., pp15-17

13   Hasluck, Paul, *Dark Cottage*, Freshwater Bay Press, 1984, p 56

14   Hasluck, Paul, *Mucking About: An Autobiography*, p 75

15   CPD, House of Representatives, 29 September 1965, p 1462

16   Bolton, Geoffrey, op cit., pp 383-84

17   Ryan, Peter, *Brief Lives*, Duffy & Snellgrove, Sydney 2004, p 92

18   Ibid., p 55

19   Hasluck, Alexandra, *Portrait in a Mirror: An Autobiography*, Oxford University Press 1982, p 128

20   Hasluck, Paul, *Diplomatic Witness 1941- 1947*, Melbourne University Press 1980, P 73

21   Ibid., p 49

22   Hasluck, Paul, *Mucking About: An Autobiography*, p 92

23   Ibid., p 146

24   Ibid., p 203

25   Bolton, Geoffrey, op cit., pp 63-4

26   *The West Australian*, 10 March 1934, p 14

27   Ibid., 12 June 1934, p 12

28   Ibid., 21 June 1934, p 19

29   Quoted in Porter, Robert, *Paul Hasluck A Political Biography*, University of Western Australia Press, 1993, p 13

30   *The West Australian*, 27 July 1936, p 16

31   Hasluck, Paul, *Shades of Darkness: Aboriginal Affairs 1925-1965*, Melbourne University Press, 1988, p 4

32   Ibid., p 68

33   Bolton, Geoffrey, op cit., p 101

34   Hasluck, Paul, *Diplomatic Witness: Australian Foreign Affairs 1941- 1947*, p 4

35   Ibid., p 23

36   Ibid., p 24

37   Quoted in Porter, Robert, op cit., p 25

38   Hasluck, Alexandra, op cit., p 161

39   Bridge, Carl, "Diplomat" in *Paul Hasluck in Australian History* (eds) Tom Stannage, Kay Saunders & Richard Nile, p 135

40   Hasluck, Paul, *Diplomatic Witness: Australian Foreign Affairs 1941- 1947,* pp 30-2

41   Porter, Robert, op cit, p 35

42   Watt, Alan, *Australian Diplomat: Memoirs of Sir Alan Watt*, Angus and Robertson 1972, p 63

43   Carl Bridge, op cit., p 134-35

44   Bolton, Geoffrey, op cit, p 155

45   Hasluck, Alexandra, op cit., pp 178-79

46   Hasluck, Paul, *Diplomatic Witness: Australian Foreign Affairs 1941- 1947,* pp 275

47   Ibid., p 175

48   Ibid., pp 289-290

49   Bolton, Geoffrey, op cit., p 191

50   *The Daily Telegraph*, Thursday 27 January 1949, p 10

51   Porter, Robert, op cit, p 71

52   Hasluck, Alexandra, op cit., p 212

53   Paul Hasluck interviewed by Gerard Henderson in 1993 for *Menzies' Child – The Liberal Party of Australia 1944-1994*

54   NLA recording of interview with Paul Hasluck, conducted by The Hon Clyde Cameron, Tape One, Side One, //nla.gov.au/nla.obj-215705852/listen/0-610~0-723

55   Henderson, Gerard, op cit., p 201

56   CPD, House of Representatives, 1 March 1950, p 247

57   Ibid., p 250

58   Hasluck, Paul, *A Time for Building – Australian Administration in Papua New Guinea 1951-1963* Melbourne University Press 1976, p 6

59   Ibid., p 5

60   Bolton, Geoffrey, op cit., p 215

61   Hasluck, Paul, interviewed by Gerard Henderson for *Menzies Child,* 1993.

62   Porter, Robert, op cit., p 91.

63   Hasluck, Paul, "New Guinea Presents Governmental Knot" and "Native Welfare Is A Big N. Guinea Task" in *The Sydney Morning Herald*, 4 August 1952, p 2 and *The Sydney Morning Herald*, 5 August 1952, p 2

64   Bolton, Geoffrey, op cit., p 230-233

65   CPD, House of Representatives, 1 September 1954, p 850

66   Beazley, K.E., *Father of The House: The Memoirs of Kim E Beazley*, Fremantle Press 2009, p 163

67   Hasluck, Alexandra, op cit, p 225

68   Hasluck, Paul, *A Time for Building: Australian Administration in Papua New Guinea 1951-1963,* p 264

69   Ibid., p 83

70   Ibid., p 84

71   Porter, Robert, op cit., p 167

72   Ibid., p 174

73   Hasluck, Paul, *Shades of Darkness: Aboriginal Affairs 1925-1965*, p 70

74   Ibid., p 85

75   Beazley, K E, op cit., pp 149-50

76   Stevens, Frank, *Black Australia*, AURA Press, 1981, p 72

77   CPD, House of Representatives, 18 October 1951, pp 875-76

78   Robert Manne, *Quarterly Essay*, https://www.quarterlyessay.com.au/essay/2001/04/in-denial/extract and Andrew Bolt, Sky News, https://www.heraldsun.com.au/news/opinion/andrew-bolt/matron-hyde-made-sacrifices-for-aboriginal-children-like-none-of-these-critics-would-dream-of-making-themselves/news-story/b5db38183f0284d093a479953a8f6b18

79   Hawke, Steve, *Polly Farmer: A Biography*, Fremantle Press, 1994

80   Boti, Tony, in *WAtoday*, 15 August 2019, https://www.watoday.com.au/national/western-australia/against-all-odds-graham-polly-farmer-sparked-a-football-revolution-20190815-p52ha9.html

81   Bolton, Geoffrey, op cit., pp 247-248

82   Ibid., p 256

83   Beazley, K.E., op cit., pp 155-156

84   Hasluck, Paul, in *News Brief* – a publication of the Institute of Public Affairs (NSW), No 2 1988

85   Allen W. Dulles, "65 Memorandum From Director of Central Intelligence Dulles to President Eisenhower", 17 April 1958, https://history.state.gov/historicaldocuments/frus1958-60v17/d65

86   CPD. House of Representatives, 23 March 1965, p 231

87   Ibid., p 241-242

88   Ibid,. p 254

89   Edwards, Peter (with Gregory Pemberton), *Crises and Commitments: The Policy and Diplomacy of Australia's Involvement in Southeast Asian Conflicts 1948-1965*, Allen & Unwin (with the Australian War Memorial). 1992, pp 361-75

90   *The Sydney Morning Herald*, 14 July 1965, p 8; *The Age*, 14 July, p 1

91   Note written by Gerard Henderson, 28 July 2025

92   *The Australian*, 31 July, 1965

93   Fairbairn, Geoffrey, "The Cairns Line on Vietnam: A

campaign of evasive obfuscation" in *The Bulletin*, 31 July 1965, pp 35-36

94   *The Sydney Morning Herald*, 2 August 1965

95   Edwards, Peter, *A Nation at War Australian Politics, Society and Diplomacy during the Vietnam War 1965-1975*, Allen & Unwin (with the Australian War Memorial), 1997, pp 69-70

96   *The Sydney Morning Herald*, 22 December 1965, p 5

97   Hasluck, Paul, *The Chance of Politics*, Text Publishing 1997, p 148

98   Henderson, Heather (ed), *Letters To My Daughter*, Murdoch Books Pty Ltd 2011, p 175

99   *The Australian*, 8 January 1968

100 Hasluck, Paul, *The Chance of Politics,* p 159-60

101 Quoted in *Paul Hasluck A Life* by Geoffrey Bolton, pp 420-21

102 Williams, Evan, "Hasluck: An intellectual in the seats of power" in *The Sydney Morning Herald,* 11 February 1969, p 4

103 Hasluck, Alexandra, op cit., p 278

104 Hasluck, Paul, *The Office of Governor-General*, Melbourne University Press 1979, p 33

105 Ibid., p 35

106 Interview with Peter Cosgrove published in *The Sydney Papers Online* Issue 52, October–December 2020, https://thesydneyinstitute.com.au/blog/peter-cosgrove-book-launch/

107 Bolton, Geoffrey, op cit, p 449

108 Hasluck, Paul, *The Office of Governor-General*, p 14

109 Hasluck, Paul, "Charteris Memo" – supplied by Nicholas Hasluck to Anne Henderson. A note (memorandum) written by Paul Hasluck on the announcement of Sir John Kerr's retirement as Governor-General of Australia.

110 Lehmann, Geoffrey, "Hasluck's Australia" in *The Bulletin*, 27 June 1970, p 53

111 Hasluck, Paul, Foreword to *Collected Verses*, The Hawthorn Press 1969, pp v-vi

112 Bennett, Bruce, "Poet" in *Paul Hasluck in Australian History* (eds) Tom Stannage, Kay Saunders & Richard Nile, p 29

113 Quoted in *Paul Hasluck A Life* by Geoffrey Bolton, p 434

114   Hasluck, Paul, *Dark Cottage*, p 41

115   Paul Hasluck, "The Aimless Society – Rethinking our future: Part One", *The Age* 8 December 1979

116   Bruce Bennet, "Poet", p 29